Chants Cockpit

Designed & Produced
by
Wilbek & Lewbar
90 Victoria Road, Devizes
Wiltshire, SN10 1EU

Author Peter Fahy
Editor Bob Wilson
Illustrations Ossie Jones
Design & Layout Emma Wilson

Printed in Great Britain

© Copyright 2000

This book is dedicated to:

To the 'Few' of the Battle of Britain and also to the pioneer pilots of the long-range Photographic Reconnaissance Unit 1940

Contents

Profile	Page 4
Foreword	Page 5
Split Second	Page 7
The Next	Page 8
The New Boy	Page 9
1940 Fighter Pilot	Page 10
The Battle	Page 12
Standby	Page 14
Scramble	Page 16
That Flaming Sun	Page 17
Two Minutes	Page 18
Sixteen Squadron	Page 19
Teamwork	Page 20
PRU Spitfire	Page 22
Photo Reconnaissance Flight	Page 24
A Met Flight	Page 25
To Him	Page 26
Forty-First Operation	Page 27
Dicers	Page 28
Cold High Flight	Page 30
Intrepid Airman	Page 31
Absent Friends	Page 32
Signed Jimmy	Page 33
Not Bloody Likely	Page 34
Nothing Personal	Page 35
Two to One	Page 36
Sweep the Skies	Page 37
Intitial Training Wing	Page 38
The Eighth	Page 39
Bless'em All	Page 40
Right to Mow	Page 41
Other Illustrated Poetry Books	Page 43

Profile

Peter Fahy was born in June 1921. He served as a pilot in the RAF from May 1941 until May 1958.

During WW2 he flew Tactical and Strategic Reconnaissance Spitfires, usually unarmed, and was awarded the DFC. From 1955-57 he commanded no. 284 Helicopter squadron during the armed EOKA rebellion in Cyprus and was awarded the AFC.

After leaving the RAF he trained as a Management Consultant, and was Director of The Anglican Stewardship Association for 21 years and served on the Council of Management of Keston College.

Foreword

In reviewing this interesting collection of poems (or CHANTS as Peter Fahy calls them) three descriptive words seemed to me to apply to them - Sincerity, Sympathy and Simplicity.

Sincerity is constantly present and stems from the author's wide experience and expertise as a pilot who is at home with every aspect of flying operational aircraft.

Sympathy is emphasised not only in his concern for his lost comrades but also for his opponents when they lost their battles and succumbed. Foes who were hated at the onset of a fight became tragic losses when they lost their lives.

Simplicity lies in the language which is descriptive and needs no embellishment. It is the language of young airmen dedicated to their work and to the serious task of defending their country.

Air Chief Marshal
Sir David Lee GBE CB

Split Second

I'd never killed before but there he was,
in that split second shimmering in my sight,
the reflex thumb depressing now because
he trespassed here and challenged me to fight -
the jabbing thumb exploded all my life,
the past and future welded into one
as joy of living quelled the passing strife
the One-o-nine exploded and was gone.
In that split second weighing birth and death,
exultant yes, yet feeling for the foe
whilst ages pass and all their time bequeath
I take a life - in that split second know
there is no absolution for this act
split second passed - intent by then a fact.

The Next

The kill next time less-conscience-stirring
experience smothers pangs of squeamishness,
consider Hitler, Goebbels, Hess and Goering,
the Hun now in my sights offends no less.
Oh! I'll be proud - 'Ace' to be my status -
but better not to judge my prey like this.
This bloody war creates a great hiatus
where man hates man - take aim you cannot miss!
Another flamer - watch your blind-spot tail
that dangerous moment after victory.
Sky stiff with haughty Huns I want to nail,
make this day's score a line in history.
How exultation overcomes the guilt!
Revenge is sweet - and thus are vict'ries built.

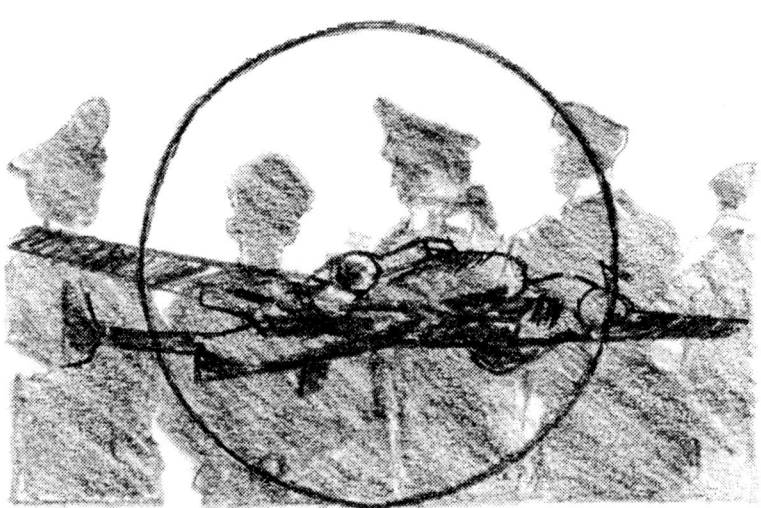

The New Boy

We flew at dawn that warm September day
whilst Jerry pounded airfields yet again
my Number Two - a new boy in the fray -
was keen as mustard, green as early grain.
The Germans went for Biggin - we were late
but found their bombers as they raced away -
I reckoned later they were but the bait
for we were bounced - how I regret that day.
I hit a Heinkel, then to my surprise -
no panic call to break, no warning shout -
my Number Two blew up before my eyes
a blast of flame - no hope of baling out.
One moment he's intent with anxious eyes
the next I break as he, the new boy, dies.

1940 Fighter Pilot

Scramble! You climb, radar-eyed,
to reach for height up sun,
a single deadly aim belied
by blithe facade of fun.
On eager, eight-gunned wings you soar
resolute that the Nazi boot
shall not reach Britain's shore.
By Dunkirk's bloody beach you shoot,
a desperate, forestalling fight
in sky that's dark with oily stains
to down or put the Hun to flight,
yet teeming, screaming, black-crossed planes
their lethal cargoes tossed
on Britain's troops, whose cause, it seemed, was lost.

To England! Nazis swarm to subjugate,
but never shall slavery suit
the Britons who - unlike good King Canute -
a paucity of weapons by their side
repelled the surging tide
of the vaunted aerial armada.
Day after day, again and yet again,
each one a Tuck or Bader,
they flew and slew - or joined the slain.
Scrambled by the bell that jangles
the taut, expectant nerve -
Booster! Climb! Deflection! Angles!
Aim! Fire! A crazy, crowded, cursing verve:
the nightmare bell, that sleep and reason mangles.

Those balmy, epic summer days
when Tom and Dick and Harry flew,
like Icarus, exultant youth,
regardless of the cost they knew
their deeds proclaimed a truth:
"Mankind is born in spirit free!"
To fly is freedom from constraints of earth;
better fly and die, than live
a slave - that's freedom's worth.
Those flaming, flying, burning days when
youth, once named remiss,
wrote in the skies that truth again,
"No greater love than this,
to save the lives of friends by sacrificing his."

The Battle

I went to my squadron anxious to please,
And keen to emulate men like these:
Ginger, Ronnie, Harry and Buck,
And the names of some who'd run out of luck.
You're twenty today? Don't worry, they said,
We'll go to the pub and drink to the dead.
With freedom at risk and our homes to defend,
We'll blast the black Nazis whatever they send.
Like knights of the air each flew his kite,
And I flew mine in a hell of a fright:
The Hun formations were thick in the sky -
My friends belted in - and so did I:
The high blue heavens a vision of hell,
Sulphur and brimstone and fire as well.

In shattering violence I fired eight guns -
A fast moving shambles - did I hit Huns?
Black crosses in range, the button you squeeze -
A split of a second - he's gone with the breeze.
Look frantically round and quarter the sky,
Not a kite to be seen - I swear - or I die.
For sprogs the first action was terribly fast,
With luck one survived, no flag at half-mast.
This trade you learn fast or don't live to learn,
Half chances of luck presume not to spurn.
No fear of death, little time for regret,
If you're lucky it's quick, life's surest bet.
Survive the day's action and then there's the Inn,
Where pints are shot down - if they've run out of gin.

Stand-by

Standing-by in the cockpit
at instant readiness
Spitfire poised like a horse on the bit
with pedigree eagerness.
Groundcrew restless standing-by
await the scramble bell
they'll fidget and sigh
and grumble like hell
'till homeward their Spitfires fly.

Telephone shatters uneasy calm
groundcrew reaction first
pilots don helmets, glove sweaty palm
as pre-battle nerves they nurse.
The duty Sergeant sprints for the bell
whose clang they anticipate
give thumbs up to groundcrew 'Contact' yell
pilots stab buttons, propellers rotate
and chocks away for the heavenly hell.

Twelve rumbling Merlins growl and fume
a gale of octane and oil
in weaving formation positions assume
wide open throttle, no coolant boil
take-off into wind all keen for the show
climb like a dingbat
wheels up as they go
battle formation no radio chat
they scan the wide sky for signs of the foe.

Angels twenty bandits in sight
horizon of threat'ning black cloud
that speeds towards them all set for a fight
a voice echoes urgent and loud
"Bombers ahead, fighters ten o'clock high -
'B' Flight upstairs - 109s - tally ho!" -
line-astern 'A' - Heinkel bombers must die
head-on they barge in midst a hundred or so
the heavens erupt and bombs fall below.

Heinkels in flames, they cut through the ranks
of Huns trailing Spits on their tails
each man for himself stick and throttle he yanks
in mad screaming skies where chivalry fails
as blasting black crosses flit through the sight
near misses and crashes too many around
suddenly anxious - there's no-one to fight
search unbelieving, not a kite to be found
re-arm and re-fuel, they're back on the ground.

Scramble

A Spitfire Squadron's panic:
Scramble! Angels twenty fast,
The cursing din satanic,
Three-o-three's and cannon's blast.

Our 'noughts' and Nazi crosses split the sky
White vapour trails and telling perspex glints,
A flamer, acrid smoke and stinging eye,
Erupting bloody blaze and lurid yellow tints.

A dangerous, cursing, reckless game for fools;
A sweating thumb that trembles on the tit,
The only rule is this: there are no rules,
Save watch your tail, some bastard's after it.

The shambles of this Piccadilly sky:
A maelstrom of metal wing and gun,
Into the vortex plunge, Tally ho! the cry,
The swastikas are swarming in the sun.

A one-o-nine flits dancing in your sights,
A jabbing burst, a flash, the bugger's gone,
A sharp look round: blue sky devoid of kites:
Five 'chutes and oily smoke, your Spit the only one.

That Flaming Sun

That flaming sun, a traitor or a friend?
One day he sides with us the next the foe
I trust no more his smiles and warming trend
he'll burn you up so watch him as you go.
The nightmare mem'ry posing as a dream
when aces high by higher ones were trumped
too late I saw their wings and cannon gleam -
from Spit aflame and breaking-up I jumped.
Oh lucky me, my flames were blown right out -
my scorching hands - can I the brolly work?
The fiendish racket stops - I spin about
and then that painful bollock-wrenching jerk.
It's peaceful now, ride down the silent sky,
the sun smiles warmly - I both laugh and cry.

Two Minutes

Two minutes say, to scramble two fresh eggs;
the Scramble Bell - the fighter pilots run,
the breakfast cook regrets their speeding legs -
their scrambled eggs, the battle has begun:
to gain that golden yolk they swiftly fly,
like lightning ripping through sporadic cloud
to streak white banners in the blue and high,
to win or die watched by the breathless crowd.
Two minutes was the scramble time decreed
to brave the Nazis in their fierce attack:
as thousands watched, 'The Few's' immortal deed
drove back the German, back and back and back:
two scrambled eggs the waiting breakfast fare -
but some grow cold before an empty chair.

Sixteen Squadron

From Northolt then to Normandy we flew,
a gaggle - we were trained to fly alone
blue Spits a tight formation never do -
and this we proved - each flying on his own.
Our advanced strip lay camouflaged by trees
a party of our groundcrew got there first
they'd braved the roads and hazards of the seas
and welcomed us with water for our thirst.
With "D" day spirit we pressed on with Ops
we also found some vintage for our cheer
then "Chiefy" said his lads would like some hops
so I flew home with Jimmy for some beer.
With ninety-gallon drop-tanks full of ale
to Normandy - thus Sixteen shall prevail.

Teamwork

Dark and dank the tarmac strips
On the wartime airfield lay
On Nissen huts dew glistening drips
In the hooded torch's ray
The Sergeant growled "Lights out" - we met -
The hut pitch-black inside
"Roll-call by trades then out you get
See every Spit D I'd."*

"Airframes?" Six the corp'ral cried
"Engines?" Six yelled an NCO
Armourers instruments bowsers replied
"You've thirty minutes," said the Sergeant "Go."
With grumbles and grunts in the dark we ran
To serve the Spitfires well
They relied on us - we were keen to a man
We'd beat the 'scramble' bell.

Off with the sheets that cover the kites
To keep cockpit and engine dry
We know the drill and we know that lights
Would attract the Hun from the sky
Trolley-accs on and chocks in place
The Fitters 2E in the cockpits sit -
All clear of the prop and its deadly trace -
Their fingers the start buttons hit.

Twelve rumbling Merlins burst into tune
Whilst riggers check every plane
The radio bods test channels for soon
They'll be up in the air again
We warm up engines examine all gear
Oxygen instruments wireless and guns

Oil pressure brake pressure perspex wiped clear
Magnetos and tyres and shells for the Huns.

On bikes or in cars or a three-ton truck
Come pilots ready to fly
They chatter and banter or brood on their luck
In a game where the luckless die
Make sure each Spitfire's in fine fettle
That everything works as it should
Our Spits and our pilots and us on our mettle
We'll prang Adolf's Nasties for good.
(*daily inspection)

PRU Spitfire

The scrambling fighter days are gone;
No cannon mars the blue Spit's line,
Armoured glass and gunsight - none:
Flush rivets aid a knot-increasing shine.

The photographic long-range Spit,
High-climbing, sleek and fast,
Unpressurised, no heater boasted it:
Its cameras breach the Nazi line at last.

A hidden petrol tank each wing contains,
More engine oil to lubricate more hours,
Pure oxygen a pilot's life maintains
Against thin air and high defensive powers.

Take time to choose the all-important maps,
Unhurried plotting of the crucial course,
A dog-leg here, diversion there, perhaps,
For speed and guile outwit opposing force.

Deep blue and silent is the stratosphere;
Bone-cracking cold above the vapour trail;
Navigate and rubberneck, the constant fear:
The sortie's lost if vigilance should fail.

Southwest Berlin's bright waters catch the eye,
Spot Brandenburg, but dream not of its name,
A dozen hostile airfields far below will try
To kill your spying, picture-taking game.

To steer a course within but one degree,
Dead-reckoning the hall-mark of the trade,
Keep swivelling eyes the enemy to see;
Fly steady, cameras on, as each shot is made.

Airfields, railways, roads, canals and beaches,
V-sites, rockets, docks, and U-boat pens;
Industry and oil the probing camera reaches,
Radar gantries, bridges, in its penetrating lens.

No secret site escapes the camera's eye,
No fighter screen deters, or heavy flak,
Dunkirk and B of B explain the why,
Whilst PRU films how we shall come back.

Cold and silent, lone and always fraught,
Yet every trip triumphant all the same,
If one exposure in the whole roll caught
The object of the sortie in one frame.

Photo Reconnaissance Flight

No guns! Dependent now on speed and height,
thick Wilton carpet clouding far below,
with eagle's eye alert - but not to fight -
to hunt the German's secrets now I go.
To Baltic isles I set my lonely course
enchanted by the universe I see ;
no war-torn world, no guilt and no remorse
but still his radar hums and fixes me.
Let stratospheres of peace exert no charm
be vigilant and wary of the Hun
whose devious air exudes a soothing balm
as clouds disperse beneath the glorious sun.
My cameras turn - and there six miles below
his airfield - and his secret weapons show.

Call "Backwash" as the Essex coast appears
and arrow down from scant cold air on high
feel raving thirst as base too slowly nears -
pure oxygen burns throat unholy dry.
Four hours since my Spitfire left this place;
from cramped seat crawl - see film mag's on their way,
stretch creaking limbs and savour freedom's space
dump helmet, 'chute, divest the yellow Mae.
Report to "Spy" who'll probe for every detail:
he offers tea - and biscuits that would choke -
when what I need - beside a pint of ale -
is good fresh air and then a pipe to smoke.
The prints are good, I feel a modest glow.
His rockets show! That's all I need to know.

A Met Flight

The Met flight seemed innocuous enough
he'd flown three tours of ops by forty-four
in U-boat land the weather forecast rough
he'd survey Kiel and Bremen, then withdraw.
Would breaks in cloud be right for operation -
for photographs from thirty thousand feet?
It's vital that we have this information
so off he went to scan the U-boat beat.
He reckoned in three hours he'd be back -
Group Captain brave - we never saw again:
some reports of fighters - nothing much of flak
as Air Sea Rescue searched his track in vain.
Control had 'fixed' him heading out to sea -
deep cold North Sea. He ditched or jumped maybe.

To Him

The Mitchells fly at height to Venlo town
the umpteenth time the bridge they've tried to hit
a tiny target as the bombs rain down
intense the flak ringed round the town and it.
And after every raid the P.R.U.
sometimes at height, more often very low
a single Spit this deadly job to do
the photo's vital - this the Germans know.
His name came up - to Venlo bridge once more
he'd been there twice before and knew it well
the massive girders and the guns he saw
with camera on he dived into that hell
into a hail of red-hot tearing flak.
To him we drink, for he did not come back.

Forty-first Operation

He'd flown on Ops for months as I well knew,
those stirring months pre- 'D' day and since then -
flown forty Ops, with twenty more to do
and now he braved Rhine bridges once again.
The Eighty-eights were wicked and well-aimed
and hit him hard as by the bridge he flew
hot stinking cordite, flaming engine maimed
pull up - bale out - the only thing to do.
He pulled the ripcord as he left the Spit
no time to count - eight hundred feet - too low
the rigging lines and parachute then hit
and snagged the tail-fin in the fierce airflow.
So strung to diving Spit he hit the ground,
so deep the grave where they his body found.

Dicers

The crewroom tense
The weather poor
The CO hurries through the door
A trip I sense
He beckons me
Four volunteers I'd like
Ops room twenty minutes hence
You and Peter, me and Mike.

The ops room charts
Marked Waal and Rhine
Four dicer trips and one is mine
And in the silence
Not a sign
Of nerves - I buried mine
The CO said low level chaps
Each pilot has his own marked maps.

The briefing short
The flight too long
From Normandy a head-wind strong
Nijmegen now lies close to port
Photo bridges
Don't get caught
By flak like midges in July
Stinging biting swarming by.

Nijmegen Bridge and Emmerich
Fly low with camera running
Blasting flak it makes you sick
But pictures should be stunning
The Spitfire now hold down on line
Right rudder so to get the shot

The bridges fill the centre fine
Out low and fast it's getting hot.

Next to Wesel fast and low
Beside the Rhine we roar
Beneath the pylon'd wires go
Switch camera on before
The bridge's ack ack guns let fly
Achtung'd to our coming
The stuff shoots up off line and high
But sharp the shell bursts' drumming.

Finished film go low like hell
Avoid Eindhoven town
Fuel low the gauges tell
It's time to put her down
The front line's past
The shell-bursts fade
Spot Douai airfield down at last
Then home to see the pictures made.

Cold High Flight

There's no publicity for us
we're undercover boys
with bottled oxygen a must
and cameras our toys.
Yes, we will fly low level too
if targets so demand
a somewhat sticky job to do
some say it should be banned.

So high we breathe on bottled gas
fly mixture-lean elastic miles
cold flights no toilet room alas
and seats too hard with dinghy piles.
We fly unheard and hope unseen
keep radio silence too
no-one knows where - or if we've been
but jolly cameras do.

And as we leave home-radar's screen
we're neither live nor dead
we are unheard, perhaps unseen
there's nothing to be said.
And when a pilot disappears
there's none knows where he went
we nurse our hopes fend off our fears
and privately lament.

Intrepid Airman

He leapt into his fighter plane
both he and it the heavens to gain,
flying such a sheer delight
especially when things went right.

So 'thumbs up' ground crew, switches 'on',
from left to right the cockpit con,
the throttle set, rich mixture 'in',
press buttons watch the airscrew spin.

Engine warm he taxies out
and weaves the long nacelle about,
for Spitfire's have a lengthy nose
under which the Merlin goes:

This hides disasters on the track
befalling those who wisdom lack
so keen to leave the earth behind:
to petrol bowser he was blind,
chewed it with his splintering prop
bold airman sad on earth must stop.

Absent Friends

Transcending circumstance and time and place,
our absent friends exert their spell;
as Omar's Finger writes the living trace,
immovable, deep etched in memorys cell.

Lone warriors these and chroniclers of war
who probed the enemy on seeing wing;
they sped his secrets past his guarded shore
to powers that would retribution bring.

They flew from Benson, Hartford Bridge and Dyce,
from Northolt, Amiens and airfields east:
time wrote the names of those who paid the price:
still youthful friends, not present at this feast.

The passing years exact their fateful toll
yet not on those we name on Honour's Roll.
Each time and place its certain memory lends:
we drink a toast to these our Absent Friends.

Signed Jimmy

They disappeared in winter forty-four -
Mike and Jimmy - just faded from the screen.
Shot down! Alive or dead? Like countless more -
the tale of P.R.U. - unheard, unseen.
The memories of youth are evergreen.

With peace declared and family life to tend
I tried reunions once or twice to see
if there I'd find at least one war-time friend
but never did - it was not meant to be.
The memories mean much to me.

Fifty-one years later came a letter,
'Have you some memory of Mike?' it said,
'his golden wedding, nothing could be better
than word from you, we both thought you were dead.'
Signed Jimmy.

Not Bloody Likely

It's all a game my boy, the loser dies
so get him in your sights and squeeze the tit
whilst up your backside keep a pair of eyes
or else the crafty Hun will pepper it.
Be sure to see them first, then check up-sun
for others will be waiting there for you
get in there fast, hit hard, then out you run
and watch your tail whatever else you do.
I ponder on those words, 'Thou shalt not kill'
and wonder on what grounds they might be void
I'll fight for country, loved ones, come what will
and question if my God will be annoyed.
The Master Race - so states the Nazi creed:
turn other cheek to them? Not bloody likely.

Nothing Personal

It's nothing personal - and this no lie.
Two nations war, all patriots involved;
this present moment either you or I
must chance to die and then one problem's solved.
My Spitfire turns inside your One-o-nine,
a climbing turn to port hauled hard and fast,
you follow, fire, your flashing tracers whine -
recoiling guns! You stall - and now at last:
it's nothing personal - I hope you see -
I'm on your tail and you're the one to go.
Pass through the veil and then enlighten me,
we diced for death, you lost, so this you owe:
you too had dreams, and you may live them now,
reach through the veil to me and tell me how.

Two To One

We've practiced scrambles 'til the Boss is pleased -
we've buckled 'chute, donned helmet, tightened straps!
The Clanging Bell - we run - the tension's eased,
away with doubts and ifs and buts - perhaps.
The battle's on and we've a job to do,
we take-off now in ninety seconds flat,
small time to think, the drill by rote run through,
and fix your mind on sterner things than that.
High flights we hunt, while Hurries stalk the rest,
we scream for height up-sun to catch the foe,
their height and numbers put us to the test,
we wait and break as they dive down and so -
a brawl - the Messerschmitts by Spits out-turned,
we lost but two, and four of theirs we burned.

Sweep The Skies

Our CO's over thirty, far too old,
knows more of horses than of aeroplanes -
'Fly by the book', he says, but we're not sold -
his line astern attacks have brought no gains.
'Fly tight in vics' - another of his tricks
that leaves us sitting ducks for ranging guns:
the outside boys the roving Jerry picks -
busy keeping station - no wary eyes for Huns!
Our twelve in tight array came on the foe -
four One-o-nines head-on face three-to-one:
their cannon-fire blasts our old CO -
four seconds flat another three are gone.
Our new young Boss holds up his right hand so -
wide finger-fours - eyes sweep the skies for foe.

Initial Training Wing

'C' Flight - Ah-ten-shun, the corporal roared,
four weeks of lectures and bullshit on the 'square':
Your country needs you - What! For this 0 Lord?
It's Wings we want, and combat in the air.
Rifle-drill, fatigues, PT and 'Who goes there?',
Airframes, Engines King's Regs and ACI
a grounding this - to help you they declare -
yours now to learn nor ask the reason why.
Learn Air Force Law - full-pack and extra drill,
we yearn for Spitfires screaming overhead
the war will end before we make a kill
then came Dunkirk - invasion next they said.
And after ITW we learned to fly -
Now disciplined to fight - to live or die.

The Eighth

The Flying Fortress bristling with guns,
each box of six like castles in the air,
I fly above them watchful for the Huns,
their target Misburg and the oil plant there:
I spot the Thunderbolts and Mustangs too
and Lightnings - zealous guards of heavy friends -
as like as not my Spitfire's azure blue
will be a target for their deadly ends.
Focke-Wulf one-nineties launch head-on attacks
against the bombers leading this array
the Thunderbolts scream down upon the packs
of German fighters in the fearful fray:
The Forts fly on, by losses undeterred,
the oil tanks burn, and victory's voice is heard.

Bless'em All

My Spitfire stood in polished gleaming pride,
her gloss a guarantee of greater speed,
the groundcrew proudly standing by her side
with matching beams - inspection may proceed.
The confidence a good mechanic gives,
to aircrew who on his work must rely,
for by his skills, a pilot dies or lives
and wins or loses battles in the sky.
Stained overalls and tools - insignia of their works,
they solemnly await my keen review -
I tell my friends, these cheerful oil-stained erks:
The bullet-holes are gone - she looks brand new;
I'll do my best to keep her that way too.

Right To Mow

One field away, beyond our airfield fence,
a two-horse team mows in a sea of hay,
each four-foot swathe releases honeyed scents
that we breathe deep as near our 'planes we lay.
This rustic scene belies our purpose there,
defenders of the farmer's right to mow -
his pastoral toil now threatened from the air,
'invasion pending' crows our Nazi foe.
The Scramble Bell destroys bucolic calm,
to Spitfires sprint - warmed-up and standing-by,
two minutes till we streak above the farm
to fly and fight for this our country's sky.
The channel ports and shipping they attack -
we beat them off but know they will be back.

THE COMPLEMENTARY ILLUSTRATIONS IN THIS VOLUME ARE BY AVIATION ARTIST, OZZIE JONES.

FOR DETAILS OF INDIVIDUAL COMMISSIONS: OSSIE JONES, 135 ASHBOURNE ROAD, LIVERPOOL, L17 9QQ, UK
TEL: 44 (0)151 727 3661

World War Two Poetry Books

Bombers'
MOON

An Anthology selected by Rod Priddle,
Air Force Poetry of World War II

ISBN 1 901284 18 2
£4.25 inc p&p

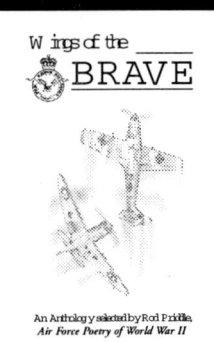

Wings of the
BRAVE

An Anthology selected by Rod Priddle,
Air Force Poetry of World War II

ISBN 1 901284 12 3
£4.00 inc p&p

To order your copy please send a cheque to **Wilbek & Lewbar**, 90 Victoria Road, Devizes, Wiltshire, SN10 IEU UK

Other Illustrated Poetry books

Other poetry books in the series:

Dreams of the Raven	ISBN 1 901284 01 8	£3.00 inc p&p
The Spirit of Christmas	ISBN 1 901284 08 5	£3.50 inc p&p
Circles of Love	ISBN 1 901284 03 4	£3.50 inc p&p
Memories of a Wiltshire Farmer	ISBN 1 901284 04 2	£3.50 inc p&p
Memories of a Wilts Farmer Wife	ISBN 1 901284 15 8	£3.85 inc p&p
Meditating Dreams	ISBN 1 901284 07 7	£3.75 inc p&p
This Wonderful World	ISBN 1 901284 06 9	£3.75 inc p&p
Life's a Laugh	ISBN 1 901284 09 3	£3.75 inc p&p
Life's Little Miracles	ISBN 1 901284 10 7	£3.75 inc p&p
Earth's Rhapsody	ISBN 1 901284 11 5	£3.85 inc p&p
Candlelight Visions	ISBN 1 901284 14 X	£3.95 inc p&p
Memories from the Attic	ISBN 1 901284 13 1	£3.95 inc p&p
Spirit of a Loving Heart	ISBN 1 901284 16 6	£3.95 inc p&p
Whispers in the Garden of Dreams	ISBN 1 901284 17 4	£3.95 inc p&p
Wings of the Brave (RAF)	ISBN 1 901284 12 3	£4.00 inc p&p
Bombers' Moon (RAF)	ISBN 1 901284 18 2	£4.25 inc p&p
Straight from the Heart	ISBN 1 901284 19 0	£3.95 inc p&p
Sentimental Journey	ISBN 1 901284 20 4	£3.95 inc p&p
Hello! Father its me again!	ISBN 1 901284 21 2	£3.95 inc p&p

If you would like to know more about our illustrated poetry books or order any of the above titles (cheques payable to Wilbek & Lewbar), then do contact us at:

Wilbek & Lewbar
90 Victoria Road, Devizes, Wiltshire, SN10 1EU, England
Tel / Fax: 01380 720271 E-mail: wil.bar@zetnet.co.uk